The
Black Words
of Green Eyes

Mia Lynn Neat

Book Printing by

FALCON BOOKS
San Ramon, California

Book Design by Mia Lynn Neat

Library of Congress Cataloguing in Publication Data
Neat, Mia Lynn.
p. Cm.
ISBN 0-9703538-0-4
Poetry, American, 2. Afro-Americans–Poetry. I. Title

First Edition

Published by
Neat Publishing
1055 Noble Isle Street
Henderson NV 89015

PRINTED IN THE UNITED STATES OF AMERICA

My Angel Lies Just Beyond the Clouds...

— Mia Lynn Neat

TO

My Mommy and Daddy, Melissa, Nila, Gina, my nieces and
nephews, my family, Marcus, my friends, and my girls who always
gave me the support and inspiration.

Thank you God for your will and faith in me.

Table of Contents

The Aftermath

Running Circles

Love

THE BLACK WORDS
OF GREEN EYES

Now right off
I know you thought of **black** words in a negative
     connotation
You thought of **black** words capturing your
     contemplation
But you didn't, for one second
Think of all the positive things that **black** beckons
The beauty that lies in the unknown
The surprise when mystery is shown
The adornment brought on by that of the crow
Who has no limits on where it can go
Just think of the thoughts that come to mind
When one wonders of the works of the watchers
Wallowing away in the wings of the waters
In a sea full of life
That ignites only during the night
A time when romance is at sight
Displaying the beauty of **black**ness
For without darkness, one cannot decipher that
     which is light
It all lies within the boundaries of **black**
The things that light has no choice but to lack
I am green eyes
The keeper of these words
I will not force upon you ideologies and isms
Rather I want you to understand and make your
     own decisions

These words belong to me
These words cannot be heard but seen
I allow them their gleam
I am lurking at all times
In the shadow or perhaps a crack
I am the green-eyed keeper and my words are
   black.

The Lord, My Savior

PRAYER

And I know the Lord will follow me
Lift me up in his arms in my time of need
Because He is the Lord
My Savior
My Freedom
My Love
So why is it so,
That pain is all I know?
My eyes are the windows,
Overflowing with raindrops like tears.
I have so many fears,
So I pray
Because I know it will get better
I have faith and I believe
Because He believes in me.

IT IS HE

Why me?
Why he?
Why she?
We continuously question the decisions of Thee
Perhaps it is ourselves that we should question
Our actions and words without discretion
It is the works of You that enable us to be
It is the words of You that enable us to see
He provides us with the tools to survive
It is up to us to use them to strive
To live and love
To be strong and wise
It is He
Who enables thee

THE WORKS

What's on your mind
When you make all things stop
I know you work in mysterious ways
Regulating things like a cop
Leaving that time open to wallow and think
My curiosity rises as I watch the anchor sink
A sudden pause
An unknown cause
Preparing for the change
But I'm unaware of my range
Yet and still the thoughts devour my mind
As all else remains behind
I'm equipping myself
As you attempt to trip myself
With the ideas that keep coming
Never an answer to be received
But I know it had to be much deeper than I
    could've conceived

I still wonder what's on your mind
When your mysterious ways are working
Keeping us unsure of what's lurking
In the times to come
Somehow the parts may be greater than the sum.

IT WAS NOT HER TIME TO GO

With siblings and children
And a family who cared
We will remember the memories we shared
Her flourishment and her flow
Her glisten and her glow
We all know
How much we'll miss her so
For we all knew it was not her time to go.

With so much life still ahead,
We hoped and prayed her life would be extended
But it seems that the Lord had other plans
For her to reach new mountains and sands.
She was needed up above,
In heaven there was a need for one more dove.
She will no longer suffer from pain,
But in all of our hearts she'll remain
She was more pure than water and snow,
So we wonder why she had to leave
For we all knew it was not her time to go.

Although the pain grows without doubt,
The sadness and mourning isn't what it's about
It's that we realize that she's resting in peace
She is living with us all, not just deceased
With every memory and every thought,
In this web of love, we'll all be caught
For, although disease was the cause she left,
It was not for the best, not an act of theft.
She is the reason that we must all go on.
We know that heaven is a place we should all go,
But no matter what, we knew it was not her time
    to go.

TO TOUCH A SINGLE SOUL

My mind is generating
All of the thoughts I've been contemplating
And I'm wondering how
I can pass on my knowledge
To those who follow
Filling up those voids that remain hollow
Minds young and agile
Hearts large and fragile
Yearning
To be learning
All of the things that help to cope
I would love to be a provider of hope
Reestablishing the faith
That has been lost and taken away
Giving stability where we once swayed
I hope that my point has been conveyed
I'm willing to pay the toll
To touch a single soul

I'm eager to supply the demand
Rather than give orders and commands
I want to be an aid
To this revolutionary crusade
Pulling down the iron curtain
That's for certain
Allowing passage
Relating the message
Conveying the point
Giving the meaning

Supplying the reason
Obtaining the goal
Just to touch a single soul

I look out into your eyes
Filled with the tears of question
Covered by the lens of life
And I am compelled to eliminate your strife
I want to influence you in every way
Give you motivation with every day
to proceed with determination
Painting you an influential illustration
About the possibilities and advantages
Rather than the obstacles and disadvantages
This craziness
And haziness
Disguised by laziness
Devours me with amazingness
And makes me want to change this
I want to capture your minds whole
Because I'd do almost anything
To touch a single soul

A Bird's Eye View

THE NEWS

What's wrong with the world today?
Crimes in our times
Dominating our lives
Now it's part of our culture
Makes me wonder what's in our future

Man, what is the plan?
I'm looking up to the Lord
Wondering what's his master plan

Floods over our lands
But I see no rainbows that assure us it's not the end

Terrorism
Filling our lives with mortality
Corrupting our economy
Making enemies in nations
Where we used to have good relations

Our kids are killing each other
We need to learn to love our sisters and brothers

Shooting, drugs, and violence
Leading us to an eternal silence

People dying to let others start living
Trying to make others see the good in giving
When we only want to live in peace

All the while our president is being accused
And abused
And ultimately refused
When he can't do his job
Because everyone has become such a critical mob
Involving ourselves
To find joy on the shelves
When all we need
Is to appreciate the seed
That gives life
But until then, we will all dwell in strife

TODAY'S WORLD IS NO DIFFERENT FROM YESTERDAY'S WORLD

In the past, we were held prisoner, as slave, and as
no good kind.
In the present, we are isolated, separated, and
considered of no good mind.
We can do our best, but the best is not good
enough
Because the color of our skin just makes them
more determined to wrap us with a cuff.
We can never be more, only of the less
And never see happiness
Today's world is no different from yesterday's
world.
This is like a cycle, but we never stay free.
We were slaves back then, until they killed some
very important men.
We showed our anger and became friends
Bad move, instead.
They say the country is free,
But where are the people black like me?
I see no black presidents, and no black leaders
We get no good jobs to support our families or
either die first
We get beat and it's no big deal
But reverse the situation and see how you feel
Today's world is no different from yesterday's
world

GIVE IT A CHANCE

How about giving hip-hop a chance?
Instead of judging it with a single glance
What you see is not always what you get
Your discrimination makes me frustrated
I feel an urging pain being aroused in my gut
It's rising from my toes to my head
Especially after all the things you've said
You make it our reality
Then you label it a practicality
Listen to what you are saying
Watch how you are behaving
This is the world we live in
And although it may be harsh
It needs to be recognized and realized
Changed and apologized
For the things we've been through
That we just want to acknowledge
You are not forced or obliged
But how about giving it a chance

Did you listen, or did you hear?
With your ears, or what they said and she said?
Because he had more money and fame
You can't stick him with all the blame
When it's his talent that paid off
And let him claim his own
While you sit back and complain and groan
Why don't you find a way to express yourself
Instead of dragging down someone else?
How about giving it a chance?
Who knows, it may be your life that is enhanced!

CURRENCY, DINERO, SCRILL, LUTE, CASH, MONEY

Currency
    Dinero
        Scrill
            Lute
                Cash
                    Money
Whatever you want to call it honey
The root to all evil
Or the stem to all success
Regardless it determines someone's happiness
They say it's the only thing that talks these days
A universal language
That's what they claim
But why does it have to be that way?
In this hour of this day
We should be past this era of shame
When the dollar determines our worth
Are we to be bought, purchased, and sold
That's not what His intentions told
Currency
    Dinero
        Scrill
            Lute
                Cash
                    Money
Boy, I tell you it's funny
Devouring our lives
While our society strives
To hold on to what little of value is left

And though money can buy that of materialistic
    origin
It cannot buy the love of our kin
The friendships made
The struggle of this crusade
The idea of the next escapade
I tell you it's all been played
Currency
        Dinero
                Scrill
                        Lute
                                Cash
                                        Money
I'm reassuring my future's staying sunny
I won't let my income be my guide
I can't continue at this stride
I refuse to let money dictate my life
I'm not going to suffer the strife
And still it remains that my visions allows me to see
That the best things in life continue to be free

TECHNOLOGY

Progression
Succession
Technology is taking over
But who says it's progress
When it's making our world a mess
Pollution
Confusion
Contaminating this nation
Trains, Plains, Automobiles
Killing their makers
And the number exceeds the bill
Computers, calculators, telephones
Making lives convenient
Delivering us from complexity
Into lives of slavery
Dependent on technology
Attention
Invention
Prevention
Detention
Our lives have been conquered
Our empires overthrown
While technology has become our clone
The answers to our questions
Ideas and suggestions
Ecology
Anthropology
Biology
All replaced by technology

THE BEAUTY OF DIVERSITY

Composed of so many elements
Accumulated in so many moments
We are so diverse in various ways
So many different characteristics
So many different shades
It is the culture and pride within us
That won't let us give up the fight without a fuss
We are strong and beautiful in every way
There are so many things that we have yet to convey

Many see us as different because of our color
But we see all mankind as different from each other
Because that's what he said and she said
But we are all the same because all of our blood is red

However, we view ourselves in a different light
We are all one, as a race, in the fight
But we too are different in our own phenotype
It's the many different shades of our creamy,
    smooth skin
It's the texture of our hair that has that thick
    swaying bend
It's the rhythm and the spirit that comes from
    deep within
It's the strong bond that will never sever between kin
It's the music that has kept us happy in every life
It has filled us with joy and delivered us from strife
There are so many things that make us run from
    each other and disperse
There are so many things that make us diverse

We are men and women
Brothers and sisters
We are thin and wide
Filled with so much pride
We are young and old
Each of our components makes us worth more
   than gold
We are like the sun and the moon
Like earth and water
Like fire and ice
Like the sea and the sky
Somehow, although we are diverse in any kind of
   weather
We all need each other and must inevitably come
   together.

If Thoughts Were Heard

AY!!!

Ay !
Is what you say to me
But why must you be such an inconsiderate dog?
What you need is a different approach
You smelly little roach!
Don't grab my arms
Is that your so-called charms?
I'm not impressed
By your speech or the way you're dressed
You are the scum of the earth
I can't even determine your worth
I am a human being
Who deserves some respect
Not some foreign dialect

My name is not Ay!
With your gold teeth
And grungy clothes
It's men like you that I continue to loathe
How about a bath and toothpaste
Any potential you could've had is gone to waste
How about a clean-cut haircut
Oh yeah! you can't spare a buck
You cheap heathen
That funky breath you're breathing
No deodorant to save your life
But it's my nose that suffers the strife
Find some ambitions and goals
I know there's something in those souls
Decaying and rotting away

Ay!
Don't complain
That's what I want to be my response everyday
Thanks for your intended compliments
But let's work on finding you some other
  supplements
How about just saying hello next time
Then perhaps I might speak to you again sometime

Realizing Me

MIRROR IMAGE

Please allow me to take you by the hand
I would like to deliver you from your fears
And take you to a place where comfort is your
  home
I would like to wrap you in my embrace
Stare into your face
And make it known what I am
I am within you
I am your inner self
I lie beyond your depths
In a sea of emotions
More vast than the oceans
Full of power and strength
I would go the greatest lengths
To devour your inner fears
Make it known throughout your years
While I tempt temptations
And exceed your greatest expectations
Still you know not that I am here
That I am you fear
I am you out on the ledge
I am your mirror image

DO THE MATH

I want to be more than what you set out for me
I want to exceed your limits
Rebel against what the world inhibits
Cause commotions
From my ambitions and devotions
Create for myself a world free of boundaries
My own queendom of freedom
Where I rule my path
It's all possible if you just do the math
I want to live in a land
Where honesty commands
Where beauty stands
Where everyone lets morals prevail
It's all a matter of time and place
Not income or race
You never know what could happen
With destiny and fate
It's all quite possible if you just calculate
Do the math

I WILL MAKE IT

Although it may seem that my life is floating down
   stream
I will find the willpower to pull myself afloat
I will regain my strength and my hope
Don't think that this is it
I will make it

You have such an affect upon me
But don't think I'll let it affect what I want to be
Give me some time to tend
I promise my heart will mend
There is nothing that will hold me down
Just wait until I come around
Don't doubt me even for a bit
I will make it

I'm fed up with crying and carrying on
It's time to move on
All the obstacles may befall me
I won't let it harm me a bit
Because I will make it

EUPHORIA

It was as if I was in a state of Euphoria
Going about my day in a way that seemed strange
Full of joy unknown to most my other days
And I began to wonder why it was so
That this was the way my life had to go
Shocked because I was happy
When each day should be this merry
No care about stress
Overflowing with happiness
Emulating this feeling of bliss
Glowing like the sun on the day after the night rain
No concept of feeling pain
How could it be that this feeling is so foreign
On cloud nine my body was soaring
And I knew
That everyone knew
Something was different about me
My sensation conveyed my glee
So I asked myself what was so different
Could it be that I was different
Then I realized what had happened
How my life was patented
I felt it through my body
That I had ended a lifelong search
Somewhat similar to the faith of the church
I had discovered and founded a treasury
The location and chest lied within me

Letting Time Go By

TIME

No time on my hands
No time on the clock
Just passing by
Leaving me distraught
With so many things to do
So many things undone
And still I've got no time
And I'm always on the run
I want to do so much
But my obligations take over
Wondering and Inquiring
How my life was taken over
The world is an enormous blur
Because I'm moving so fast
And there seems to be no cure
For all the things in the present I didn't finish in
    the past
This procrastination is devouring my life
Now my world that was once filled with glory is
    emulating strife.

WHILE I DON'T EVEN ASK MYSELF WHY

All the while I'm thinking
That I'm facing
Something different than I'm embracing
Time in my life passes me by
While I don't even ask myself why

Things are happening
It's all quite baffling
What is it that I will encounter next
Will it be revealed through my text
Or perhaps on an expedition
To be discovered upon the following rendition
Of authoring my own edition
To be added to the series of volumes
Created for my lyrical tumes
Preserving the words of my tongue
For later use by my daughter and son
I know that I'm here for a greater purpose
Contributions made to the whole
But what is the fee for the toll
At the expense of letting life pass me by
While I don't even ask myself why

Perhaps if I stopped to smell the air
To feel the fluff in the clouds
The splendor in the grass
The shine in the sun

The wonder in the wind
The fertility in the earth
The fluidity of the water
The blaze in the fire
And the expression of creation

I might not be limited by contemplation
But set free by will
Just by lifting up the window from its sill
And finally when I notice the world by my side
I'll be enjoying myself
While I don't even ask myself why

ANOTHER DAY, ANOTHER NIGHT

Another day
Another night
Passing me by
Out of my sight
Leaves falling
Phone's telling me someone's calling
But I can't initiate any moves
I'm paralyzed by the grooves
Dancing in my heart
As it palpitates
My mind generates
Non-stop ideas
Continuous thoughts
I'm filled with knowledge
Information you can't get from college
It's nourishment for my body
Food for my song
Playing me tunes
And I'm singing along
Not with words
But with my motions
It's a kinetic love potion
Sending off vibes
Initiating tribes
Casting spells
Releasing us from our stressed-out cells
And there's so much going on

We're grooving 'til dawn
And yet another day
And another night passes me by
It's out of my sight

DADDY'S LITTLE GIRL

Daddy , wake up
I'm still here
I know you've been searching for me everywhere
But I didn't leave
I've been here all the time
My presence is eternally in your heart and mind
I know that it's hard to face
But I need just a little space
I need a little room to grow
I must learn on my own to reap and sow

You've done your job
And a job well done that is
Now I'm learning to apply the knowledge you've
    given me
Now you've passed on that magical key
That seems to open doors when opportunity
    knocks
I have the master key to all of the locks

I know it hurts to reminisce on all of our memories
Thinking back to all the times we had
All the time I was the shadow of Dad
Wanting to be just like you
Doing everything you'd do
Saying everything you'd say
And all the times we'd play
But I'm just letting you know that it doesn't have
    to end

There are still memories left to make
And helping hands to lend
Stories to share and tell
More letters in the mail
So just open your eyes a little wider

Now it's plain and obvious to see
Daddy it's me
The one that no one can replace
Your own little treasured pearl
It's Daddy's little girl!

JOURNEY

Picture in your eyes a never-ending road
Leading to a place never heard of, a place untold
Initially approaching it caused so much fear
Now upon departing it we drop a tear
For this road, although it was long
Was full of laughter, friends, and song.
Along this road there were many hurdles to
    overcome
Arduous for many and easy for some.
All the memories, by our heart that we have kept
Caused us to grow, allowed us to become adept
It's not about who finished first or who finished
    last
It's about who made a future and who got through
    the past
It's about the hard work put in
The helping hands that we lend
The relationships we've made
The paths we've laid
Commending one another
Becoming sister and brother
The songs of bitter joy brought to mind
The good and bad times we must leave behind
For this road that we've traveled
Is finally unraveled
This road is full of new people
Full of graduates and beginners
This road is full of winners
A winner is in the mind, body, and heart

It is more than a piece of art
It's in the method of moving
The sensation of grooving
The feeling it brings
And the reward that sings
It's more than a temptation
But the accomplishment that takes you to a whole
    new level of elevation
For a winner is made of many ingredients
It is a person guided by expedience
Down the many roads and paths of each journey.

The Aftermath

A PAGE IN THE HISTORY BOOK

I've got things on my mind
And goals to pursue
I've got so much ahead of me
So give me a good reason, I should worry about
    you
You think my life is a gift for you
Well, I think you're in the wrong gear and you need
    to shift
I can't continue my life
Sitting at this bus stop
Waiting for a bus that's broken down
I've got two feet that will help me get to the next
    town
I may be new at finding me
But at least I know now that I'm on the right track
And I'm heading there fast
Leaving behind the troubles of my past
Don't say that I'm running away
Because there's only so much time in a day
And I've got to finish
The items on my list
I can no longer aim to please
Those who cannot be appeased
I tried to pacify the continuous demands
But it's just a new phase in my life that has
    stronger commands
I'm elated to have come to terms
With where I stand
And knowing where I'll land

And understanding the meaning behind my plan
It's funny how things seemed content
When at night I was the one who had to repent
And ask forgiveness from myself
For allowing me to be exploited
For allowing me to be degraded
For allowing me to be contaminated
By these pollutions that challenge me on the daily
I'm a lady
And I've found my own story

I DIDN'T KNOW IT 'TIL YOU WERE GONE

How much I miss you
How much I cared
The heartache I suffered
The tears that I spared
How much I loved the sound of your voice
Why didn't I do something when I had a choice
I didn't know it til you were gone

All I see is your face
And your color is so vivid
All I feel is your presence lingering throughout my
    space
You are full of love and so livid
And when I think of you
From sunlight til dawn
It is when I remember us
That I realize that I didn't know it til you were
    gone

Only when I know
That I can live again
Is when my pain and heartache from the thought of
    you will end
I reminisce on our memories
Thinking of all the things you did
That made me hate and love you concurrently
It is the thought of you

That allows me to go on
And now I know I'll always have you near
But I didn't know it til you were gone
I wish I would've told you sooner
But I didn't know it til you were gone

IN MY HEART

How could it be
That I did what's right for me
When the pain inside
Seems so great
There's just no way to deny
There's just no way to debate
Although I've gained some integrity
And I may have gained some pride
I only feel that I've lost all the love inside
I only feel that It's pain I can't disguise
I miss you so much
I miss the warmth of your touch
I wish you were here
To wipe away my tears
I've lost my best friend
The one who I loved most
But inside I'm longing to be in your embrace
I love you with all of my heart
But I knew it was time for us to part
It feels as if you've died
Because I'm left with only memories inside
I'm the one who's mourning
I'm the one left soaring
Now you live only in my heart
It makes me cry to think we had to part

MY LIFE HAS NO MEANING

My life has no meaning
It's like I'm walking through the world of a blank
   picture
Searching for something that matters to me
I see nothing and no one
Like I'm awaiting a death
That's taking it's slow time
So that I may suffer
There is a sense of muteness
A sense of lacking visuals
Someone has assured me being miserable

But why would I take the life that has once
   brought me love?
If I did take it, God would surely prohibit me from
   going above

So I sit and cope
In a life without love and hope
Waiting for this so-called drastic change
While my life continues to have no meaning.

MY TURN

I stand portraying myself to be solid and strong
When my insides are empty and hollow
I feel so incomplete and all things feel wrong
I don't know how I'll go on
I'm trying to keep myself busy
So that I don't have to think about you
I've watched more movies than blockbuster can
   hold
I have become a lifeless mold
I'm a once-loved has been
All songs seem to relate
And everywhere I look I see couples in love
And all I can do is think back to our memories
And wonder when I will have my turn in endless
   love

IF YOU REALLY LOVED ME

If you really loved me
You would've let me know
You would've bluntly let it show

Stop denying it inside
There's no way to hide
The way you feel about her
So listen up sir

I'm tired of your lies
Your charm and your disguise
Telling me that I could be number one
Just so I would hold on
Throwing a fight when I needed to say good-bye
Making me feel guilty
For wanting to be free
Of the pain and agony
You caused
There ought to be laws
Against your kind
Playing so many games with my mind
But whatever you say
Is contradicted by your chest
Because it's written all over
In plain ink
Exactly what you think
You say she doesn't complete you
Then why do you rush home to call her on the
    phone

But you didn't care that you left me alone
You took her to the show
But what you didn't know
Is that I'd know
You bring her around
Being careless about how I feel
What you really need to see
Is if you really loved me
With me is where you'd be
I love you and I'm sorry
This is the way it has to be
But now I see that you
Would've proved it already
If you really loved me

WITHOUT LOVE

I'm sitting here looking around
At the sight of everyone in love
No matter what direction
There are non-stop signs of affections
Plaguing my mind
With the idea that there is no other route
Telling me that love is a priceless loot
Currency for life
And without we die
I'm under the impression
That there is no alternative
No other options
Making me feel obligated to make the love
    adoption
Holidays in honor of this so-called ideal
Full of love, lust, and sex appeal
Cards, candy, and romantic dates
Is this nature or simply fate
I can't seem to get by this goal
To be in love and remain that way until I'm gray
    and old

So is this real?
Is this the only deal?
Then why am I not in love?
What are the requirements?
How do I earn the others' sentiments?
If I'm not in love
What will my life be made of?

Sadness and pain?
Loneliness, living in vain?
Does it matter?
Who am I waiting for?
Will he walk through my door
Unexpectedly?
So suddenly?
What is my life without love?

I AM NO LONGER HUMAN

The windows to my soul are filled with rain
The home of my soul feels like it has been slain
The engine to my machine has been broken down
The object has been outlawed from this town

I am no longer human, nor humane.
I am no longer sane, nor insane.
I am an object, inanimate, and without life
All feeling has been severed with a knife.

I have been completely transformed
Why was I not even informed?
It seems as though this body that I call a home,
Has left me full and pain and all alone
The windows to my soul, which we call eyes
The rain is the tears that come when told lies.

This engine in my machine which I call a heart
Will soon be forced to depart
I am no longer human.

OPEN HEART?

Why is the world black,
When I am so blue?
Why has life died,
When it's my feelings I can't hide?
Why am I so baffled from deep within,
When I have neither greatly achieved nor sinned?
There is a claim that love is all we need
Then why is it so hard to find this seed
Of love that will blossom to all lengths?
It will take you from being weak to various
    strengths.
I wonder if I shall ever let my heart pour again.
For all the pain that was caused, leaves me
    questioning if I still can.

But this feeling is not felt solo,
Many must let things go with the flow.
But we must realize that there's always a shoulder
    to cry on
Sometimes we must laugh instead of mourn
For all of lifes' collisions and dents,
We must realize the explanation of those solo
    footprints.

THE VERGE OF TEARS

I'm on the verge of tears
Hiding from my greatest fears
I can't seem to face
The fact that we run a different pace
You're in the fast lane
And I'm strolling slow
Denying my feelings
Climbing stairs towards glass ceilings
I thought you were within my grasp
But something broke the clasp
I thought that we could be one
But you forced us to be done
And now all I can do is question
Listen to suggestion after suggestion
Wonder what's my fate
To indulge in love or hate
So I'm walking around on the verge of tears
Admiring the lives of my peers,
That lack this overwhelming strife
Awaiting a new beginning to my loveless life.

Running Circles

UNREQUITED LOVE

So I packed my bags and I was ready to go
Then suddenly you realized that you had feelings
    to show
When I was giving you unconditional love
You practically gave me a push and a shove
To remove myself from your sight
I was always in some situation of blight
It seems my specialty is unrequited love
One after another a dog disguised as a dove
Reeling me in like a fish on a rod
Like I was his slave and he was my God
I gave all that I could give
No longer in this way could I live
Accepting less than I deserved
From now on my love is set on reserve
You're playing with my emotions
Keeping me under spells with all of your charming
    love potions
Knowing exactly what it is I want to hear
Slicing my heart with your selfish sear
And you ask me why I'm leaving
Because I can't take anymore of your deceiving
I'm tired of your lies
And you're wandering eyes
That curious mind
I'm leaving it all behind
It's too late
To try to compensate
For the manhood that you lack

I've got myself headed on the right track
Anywhere you aren't seems best to me
Because love made me blind
But now I can see
Quite clearly from your view
That the only person you care about is you
So although it may be so
That this is the route I had to go
To realize that I'm worth so much more
There are many roads that I have yet to explore
I'll spend the rest of my life trying to get rid of
This curse I have of unrequited love
Before I allow you to hurt me again
Know that I have will, stronger than iron and I
    refuse to be had

MAZE

This maze that I'm running through
Doesn't seem to have a way out
Because I've done everything I can do
I've cried my last cry, and shouted my last shout
You keep luring me to dead ends
While I'm accepting the bate
I must have mistaken you as one of my friends
But now I realize that it must have been a
    coincidence and far from fate
I'm tired of taking the run around
I'm exhausted from this game
I'm skipping this town
And losing this name
I'm no longer yours
Nor anyone else'
I belong to myself
I makes my own choices
I invented my own way out
And kicked down the doors
I'm finished with you demands and all of your
    chores
I'm free to roam
Free to be on my own
I'm finding my own home
I'm giving back the one I had on loan
It's a little scary here
Not knowing what it's like without you
But I'm erasing those fears
And I'm celebrating my blues

Don't worry about me
I'll get along fine
I'm still able to see
The sun is my guide

FED UP

I have come back to you time and time again
But the crime you've just committed is definitely a
  sin
I'm tired of your shit
And I'm just not putting up with it
I believed you because I wanted to
But now there's just no denying what I have to do
I'm leaving your ass cold in the gutter
And I don't want to hear any of those lies you
  choose to utter
You said you love us both and together we
  complete you
But I'm forcing you to indulge in the truth
You can't have your cake and eat it too
Because now it's your chance that you just blew
Now you've got her name written all over your
  chest
And now I'm leaving this love in the past with all
  the rest
You may be able to fool some
But you just lost this one
I'm not sitting here waiting on anything
Now it's all said and done

A Time Like This Time

You knew the way I felt
But since we weren't communicating under the
    belt
You wanted to close the book
And put it back on the shelf
But see, that's OK with me
Because as far as I'm concerned
This is black history
Now you've got me studying and learning
You've got me sincerely yearning
To gain some knowledge about you and your kind
How you continue to survive
In a time like this time
I'm more curious than George
This fact I can't even forge
I want to know the secret
I want to know how you keep it
Going and Going and Going
'Til it's gone
And yet you get to determine when it's been too
    long
You're the one who's been untrue
While she's the one who ends up blue
Because all you've got on your mind
Are quickies and one-night-stands,
How much of a man you are,
How much props you'll get,
And who's the next victim to get lit
With your blazing fire of lust

Devouring every bit of love and trust
That women ever had for you
What do you expect them to say and do
What's really sad is those few
Who happen to be men too
Take the rap and reputations
For those people who insist on corrupted relations

And still I wonder how you survive
In a time like this time
It's about time for your ship to sink
Your kind should be extinct
Putting your jewels
In every treasure around
Because you think it's worth something
Well it's worth more than you think
Children unwanted and unprepared for,
Diseases with injuresome and fatal outcomes,
And a life of solitude.
I hope it's worth that much to you
Just to feel what you feel
In the spur of that moment
To get some temporary satisfaction
Based purely on attraction
I don't think I'll ever know how you and your kind
    survive
In a time like this time.

EMOTIONAL BALL

I'm an emotional ball
Rolling throughout the circle of life
Never knowing where it began
And where it will end
Tears of sadness
Tears of joy
A yell of laughter
A feeling of being annoyed
Feeling of happiness
Full of gladness
I'm screaming and yelling
Listening and Telling
Smiling and crying
Angry and denying
All the while I'm
Being rounded into an emotional ball
Awaiting the great fall

LOST

In your eyes, in their deepest depths
This is where I am lost.
A whole new world,
Full of mountains and rivers, that I'm ready to
    cross.
When I see your face,
My thoughts become misplaced,
My heart is open for you to see.
It's more than a coincidence that only you have the
    key.
I am like water; what you see is what you get.
I am a candle waiting for my flame to be lit.
I am lost in all the places you conceal.
I am ready to love, kiss, and feel,
But I am lost and ready to be found.
With your arrival, my time has come around.
I am ready to become lost in your love.
I know that it must have been sent from above.
You are my angel, for you caressed me with your
    wings.
Whenever I feel your loving embrace,
My heart always sings.
I am ready to give my burdens a toss.
I am ready to go with you and become lost!

DISTRACTIONS

I know what I'm supposed to be doing
And it's my future that I'm screwing
But it's my emotions taking over
Not even the luck of a four leaf clover
Can help me back on the right track
Some might wonder if I were on crack
Being so easily distracted
When my paths have been secured
I wonder if I'll ever be cured
From this sickness caused by the need for love
Especially when I have so much to accomplish
    before being beamed up above
Some way or another
My life is distracted by my need for a lover
It gives me reason to go to class
It makes me forget all my lessons learned from the
    past
All my good judgment seems to be swayed
Whenever I smell the aroma of cologne freshly
    sprayed
It's more than a distraction, it's more like a spell
That has been cast upon me and is gradually
    dragging me to hell
It's stronger than any love potion
Because it has involved my every emotion
This distraction has taken every fraction
Of my passions and attractions
And made a whole distracted person out of me
But maybe one day I'll concentrate and find sense

Hopefully, not at my expense
Without the pain and fear
Perhaps one day the need for these distractions
will become clear.

Love

HOW DO I KNOW I LOVE YOU?

How do I know I love you?
It's quite clear to me now
That my heart was awaiting the right moment
To let you know what I felt
Hoping not to get hurt again
It's simply got to be a sin
The number of times this heart of mine has longed
    for relief
It just wasn't in my beliefs
That love could be in the cards
It's too hard
To fully believe this is real
I don't even know if my heart can feel
It's numb from the pain
It's been slain
I can't if it'll be the same
But I believe in you and me
I have to see
If this is what my heart's been waiting on
Or is all the love gone?
You've showed me so many new things
I could never accept less than you've introduced
    me to
It's all about you
You've blown away the competition
There could be no repetition
Of all the possibilities there for me
It's all about what we could be

How do I know I love you?
You inquire of me sincerely
Unaware of my roots
I tell you I just know
Answering with whatever suits
Then it dawned on me how I came to know
It's the little things and the signs
That make me realize
How I know I love you
You hadn't been gone for a day
When I tried to hide
The fact that I missed you
I remembered every word you'd say
And there's nothing I'd rather do
My mind's on the thought of you
It's waking up in your arms
Being subjected to all of your charms
It's your face being the last thing I see when I
  leave
And the first thing I see when I arrive
Arguing just to make up
Others wondering what's up
But it's a you-and-me thing
I don't think they could even comprehend
What it is that we've got going on
It's knowing you care
Knowing there's nothing you wouldn't spare
To spend your free time with me
It's knowing here in my arms is where you'd
  rather be

It's knowing I'm your queen and you're my king
It's that feeling that inspires me to sing
To write and express all of me
I can't begin to explain all of the things that define
All of the things that let me know that I've found
   my find
If I could
I would
Spend every waking minute
With my prince indeed
Just with one touch
When you feel my hands clutch
It's a given what I feel
My emotions begin to erupt
I'm feeling abrupt
Making my body tingle
I don't ever again want to be single
Just being with you is enough
And that's how I know I love you so much!

LOVING

My heart is yearning
And all of my body is screaming
As all of my limbs
Are dying for affection
Let's make the connection
As one, our bodies will move
We're in that erotic groove
'Cause we're in that magnetic field
Now all of my thoughts must yield
Because I'm starting to fantasize
Now that I've got my eyes on the prize

What a reward when we catch eye contact
Now I feel reassured of all that confidence I lacked

Our bodies are talking
Although our lips haven't moved
Ooh, you are so smooth
With such subtle gestures
We have a complete understanding
Of the messages we're sending
And where our hearts will be landing
I want you to be close
Squeeze me so tight that I feel comatose
Hold me in your arms
Unleash all of your sugar coated charms
Push me and Pull me
Call out my name
Tell me you love me
And don't say it with shame
Kiss me on every part
Don't forget to touch the heart

ROMANTIC NIGHTS

The moon glistens
While the night listens
To the sounds of crickets chirping
Never knowing what may be lurking
The beauty of the darkness
With stars shining bright
A warm breeze blows
To create the air of romance
Thoughts of dance
Candle lit dinners
The light of evening gown shimmers
Prancing through the night
Only love seems to be in sight
Roses in hands
Music of bands
Caressing and cuddling
Whispering and holding
Only love is molding
Until the morning lights
These are the things that occur on romantic nights

IF ONLY THE HEART COULD SPEAK

I am weak
Yet my affect is stronger
I pump life
Yet I emulate strife
So tender
So easily hindered
Large in many aspects
Abused and deprived of respect
Necessary for life to go on
Yet with my presence, pain is born
If only a shield was built to protect
My existence, from this everlasting heck
I have my own language, my own dialect
That communicates by means of the body to the
   opposite sex
I give all the precious gifts that money cannot buy
Love is my specialty that I cannot deny
It takes so much willpower for me to listen to the
   brain
But it is always his advice that leaves my messages
   slain
So many tears of my soul drown the world with
   sorrow
In hopes that the sun will return tomorrow
It brings humor to imagine all the unnecessary
   pain I endure

So silly of me to take so much pain in exchange for
   an unworthy adventure
But in the end I am ready to love again
Because I am unconditional, in a never-ending
   search, that leaves me prepared to suffer,
Unless love is what I have found in the end!

ANSWER TO MY PRAYER

So I've wished and prayed
For a love of my own
Something to me that was unseen and unheard
Everlasting and unconditional
Forever and mutual
And though I never thought my prayer would arrive
Here you stand in front of me well and alive
Staring into my eyes
With feelings undisguised
Here to prove my worst fears wrong
There you stand handsome and strong
With intentions sincere
The answer to my prayer is here

SOMETHING TO YOU

What is it about me that intrigues you,
                deceives you,
                        and exceeds you?
Why am I the one you chose,
                you know,
                        and you loathe?
Who am I to you,
                through you,
                        and to behoove you?
How can I fear you,
                be dear to you,
                        and be near you?
When can I face you,
                lace you,
                        and embrace you?
Where can I feel you,
                appeal to you,
                        and conceal you?
These are the questions that run through my mind
Over time and time
Is it a crime?
I feel like a mime
No words, just action
Limited by distractions
Overflowing with passions and attractions
I'm volcanic
Going manic
Throwing me into a panic
Over these questions in my head

All the things we said
Thinking of where we're being lead
I can't help but wonder about this craze
Am I in a maze?
Or is it just a phase?
That I must embrace
With patience instead of haste
Or is it just a waste?
You've got me going insane
Filled with pain
Feeling slain
Calling out your name
Like some simple dame
Is this just a game?
So tell me again who,
              what,
                  when,
                     where,
                        why,
and how I came to mean something to you?

WHEN YOU LEAST EXPECT IT

When you least expect it
You'd be surprised what could happen
Dreams could come true
Prayers could be blessed
You could be granted happiness
Love could appear
Perhaps before your eyes
In the future, who knows what lies

When you least expect it
You'd be surprised what could happen
Though you may be sad and in the dumps
That could've happened for a reason
Perhaps it was the love season
You may be down and feeling blue
But Prince Charming may come along to comfort
   you

When you least expect it
You'd be surprised what could happen
The sun may rise on a different side
So that shade may be what the trees provide
The wind may be still
Yet the grass may sway
So on your picnic you'll have a romantic stay
Love may be in the air
When you are the least aware
Just look around and you may notice a handsome
   stare

Full of good intentions and honest desire
You never know when a spark could lead to a blaze
  of fire
And still the fact remains

When you least expect it
You'd be surprised what could happen

WHO SAID TIME COULD MEASURE LOVE?

Who said time could measure love?
I thought it was a gift willed from Him up above
But let me know if I stand corrected
Because the mysterious ways were there last time I checked it
Allowing love to come when you least expect it
When it's staring me in my face, am I supposed to reject it?
I can't seem to grasp this illogical concept
Because if love knocks on my door, I'm going to accept it

Who said time could measure love?
Something more rare than the white dove
It has flown into my life
And perched in my heart
It's simply something I can't resist
I'm feeling compelled to persist
I know there's got to be a reason that it has befallen me
Is it temporary or is it my destiny?

Who said time could measure love?
You've got me wondering what you're thinking of
Is there a certain amount of seconds, minutes, hours, days
Before I'm supposed to take part in this ultimate gaze?
Delivering me a view of what happiness could be
Waiting for this so-called instant in history
That informs us of the difference
Between the spur of the moment and long-lasting eternity
I can't even seem to fathom this hidden meaning
When something feels right
But has the possibility of being wrong

All the while my contemplation
Overflows my mind with ideas of temptation

Who said time could measure love?
I can't agree with what you're thinking of
How is it that this thing can feel utterly perfect?
It's just something I would never expect
Being used to waiting, playing, staying
Facing the possibility of displaying
What lies behind my shield
Learning to play the field
So I can weigh my options
But why should I have to make these adoptions
Of something that takes so long
All so I can keep it going strong
So they say that all good things are worth waiting for
And it's true of the object that one adores
But what if by some strange chance
There was an opportunity to take a glance
At what lies within the future
Which beholds the ability to lure
And reel in all of my dreams
And all that my heart deems
To be necessary for ultimate joy
Not just an intimate toy
But a partnership in glory
And the first line on the page of what is to become our
    never-ending story
So what remains the question at hand
Is
    Who said time could measure love?
      I don't think I'll ever understand what you're thinking of

BUTTERFLY

Initially you are just a creature that is unique within
Although you do not stand out, you show potential again and
   again
You are beautiful within, which is what really counts
Your kindness and joy releases in abundant amounts
But it is you that I see whether you are present or in my
   mind
You are not hard to find yet you are one of a kind

However, it is the potential that you behold
That makes you worth more than silver and gold
So, as time is allowed to progress
It is ultimately beauty that you possess
It is your gift for all that you have had to endure
Now you are beautiful and now you are pure
It is inevitable that you must spread your wings and fly
So it is with pain that I release you to soar higher than the
   sky
But I know that if you have love within your heart for me
Time will tell you that here is where you ought to be
If we are meant for one another
Then we will meet again to be together forever at one time or
   another

So butterfly spread your wings
Learn and experience new things
And if time permits with permission from the man up above
It will be me and you forever in Love.

CLUB SCENE

Endless lines
People of all kinds
Waiting
Anticipating
The good times to be had
Trying to keep up with the latest fad
Dressed to impress
Hoping the love search will end in success
Paying money every weekend
Just to put that search to an end
And that's what's funny about the club scene
I know you know what I mean

Men ready to poke up against women
Women doing things that we all know is a sin
It's something about the environment
That makes people do things they'll resent
Dancing close
Simulating the real thing
Just because on their finger there's no ring
Thinking something changed at the club this week
That wasn't there last week
The air is hot and humid
The lights are low and dimmed
The music plays the songs in our hearts
With every beat someone jump-starts
The groans and moans
Of someone's' hormones
Being aroused on the dance floor

Boy it's a shame seeing some on all four
Doing dances that weren't made for public
People are really getting back
Like they were performing ceremonies and rituals
Almost like they were vigils
It's just normal seeing things you've never seen
It's all part of the club scene

HOW DO YOU LOVE A BLACK MAN?

How do you love a black man?
How do you love a black man?
I'll say it again 'case you didn't understand
How do you love a black man?
Simple you say?
Well, I beg to differ
I've gained some experience
And now I've made a little sense
It's quite simple, though it may be at your expense

First off, you should be down to chill
And then maybe you'll keep from going down hill
Just be cool like one of his boys
They do like things other than sex toys
You've got to be on the level
Capable of understanding
Don't be gullible or demanding
They like these subtle things
Not someone who clings

They've said it before
The way to his heart is through his stomach
So make your way to the kitchen
And start acting on that fix
Make all the things his taste buds desire
Not too much spice, not too much fire
Go on be brave
Make everything he craves
From breakfast to dinner

His resistance is getting thinner
Then before you know it
With this simple tempting aroma
He's sprung off you like a spell in a coma

But it's too bad that it's not just that simple
You have to be sure not to worship him like the
  gods in the temple
Turn this picture around
Help him pick his bottom lip up off the ground
Because when he sees you
It should be love at first sight
The way you bat your eyelashes
Make sure nothing clashes
The way your body talks to him
Make sure the lights aren't the least dim
So he won't miss a glimpse of your tenderness
Wishing he could speak
But he's been speechless ever since he got a peak
At what you've got to offer
Legs that talk with every step you walk
And with each sway of your hips
You'll catch him licking his lips
As his eyes move up to your breasts
He wouldn't ever think of looking at anyone else
With sensuality he's imagining your erogenous
  zones
He is definitely assured that there could never be
  any clones
That could duplicate what he's just laid eyes on
And then when he finally reaches your eyes

He knows within, there must be a surprise
Lurking in your eyes of mystery
Because he has never met a woman like you in all
    of his extensive history
Then you gave him a wink
He almost lost his balance because he didn't even
    take time to blink
But everybody knows that looks can be deceiving
It could never be that easy, even with all that
    you're achieving
There are so many things we haven't even covered

It's all in the mind
Where are the answers we are looking to find
It's these games we play
On each and everyday
To see who has the power
To dominate the others' willpower
Who can be more manipulative
All the while being inventive
Who gains the trust
At the expense of the others' lust
Changing what's fake into something real
With a pinch of attitude and cup of sex appeal
Using what he wants as ammunition
To change and alter his every decision
See it's all in the games of the mind
That determine the line between lust and love
It's just something that some take advantage of
But some end up tangling with the devil
But you know what?
I'm not even on that level

And last but not least
In all the tips that we've gained
There is one that ranks at the top of the game
Getting him to say the words
We thought we learned it
When we found out about the bees and the birds
The words give new meaning
To relationships that are leaning
Yearning to be stabilized
Something they don't seem to realize
Without the words, it's just talk
Without them, let him walk
He's got to learn to make a choice
If he's a real man, let him use his voice
Men without words are just babies
And we are not their guardians or their mamas
That's someone else's problems
So let him admit
Otherwise, stop putting up with his shit
So you ask me
How do you love a black man?
Well, how do you love a black man?
That's the response I have to give
It's different in all the lives we have to live
I'll say it again case you didn't understand
How do you love a black man?
Simple you say
Well, I beg to differ.

MON AMI

Quel homme
Il est tres intelligent
Mon ami est un beau garcon
Il me donnes beaucoup de amour
Il a mon coeur

Il est mon ami comme ma soeur
Je lui regarde dans la fenetre
Son amour me fait mal a la tete
Il a l'air parfait
Mais Il est un homme seulement
Mais Il est mon ideal homme vraiment
C'est les yeux brun
C'est le color jeune
C'est la bouche
Que tres rouge
C'est vous que j'aime
Parce que vous etes mon ami.